Bearded Dragons

Everything About
Purchase, Care,
and Nutrition

Manfred Au

BARRON'S

Contents

Typical Bearded Dragons

Bearded dragons are no longer just a secret tip among reptile keepers. There are good reasons for the ever-increasing popularity of these lizards: their amazing friendliness toward humans, their fascinating behavior, their bizarre appearance, and last—but not least—their adaptability, which make them ideal terrarium inhabitants.

Peaceful and Adaptable

In contrast to many other lizards, bearded dragons become very peaceful, and often virtually tame. They let themselves be picked up and can actually be held. Many of them even seem to enjoy direct contact with humans. Above all, they have retained their original behavior. With all that, they provide their owners with extraordinary and fascinating observations, which amaze experienced terrarium keepers even years later.

Suitable Also for Beginners

Bearded dragons are native to the arid regions of Australia. They have become perfectly adjusted in terms of their body structure, physiology, and behavior to their hostile environment. This extraordinary adaptability makes them ideal terrarium inhabitants, which can even be kept by beginners without any problems.

More and More Popular as Pets

Of all bearded dragon species, *Pogona vitticeps* and *P. henrylawsoni* are the most important ones for the terrarium hobby: both species have been kept and bred in captivity for more than 25 years. Over the years, breeders have produced more and more spectacular color forms (morphs) of *Pogona vitticeps*. However, this has not affected the popularity of the more insignificantly colored, original form, which is nowadays the most commonly kept reptile species. Of course, bearded dragons have certain requirements for their maintenance, the furnishings of the terrarium, its climate, and their diet. Anyone intending to keep these reptiles should be familiar with their behavior, in order to prevent tragic accidents right from the start. They can be friendly and peaceful toward their keepers, but rough and abrasive among each other.

Survival Artist in the Outback of Australia

Bearded dragons live in the semi-deserts, steppes, and dry forest areas of Australia that cover the largest part of the continent. They are absent in the wet north, in the extreme southeast and southwest, as well as in Tasmania.

With Beard and Cryptic Appearance

The *Pogona* lizards are a very successful group of reptiles in that they are superbly adapted to extreme heat and dryness.

Genuine only with a beard. A characteristic feature of all *Pogona* lizards is a spiny pouch under the jaw that can be extended outward into a fan, by means of the hyoid bone apparatus. This "beard" display renders the head of these lizards much larger than they actually are.

Thick skin. The skin of bearded dragons is extraordinarily thick and robust and protects against UV radiation as well as against injuries.

This common bearded dragon (*Pogona vitticeps*) has fled up a dead tree and is displaying for the photographer.

Heat compensation. Morning temperatures in the Australian outback can be quite low, and so bearded dragons need to bask in the sun to warm up. For that, they darken their coloration to ensure that heat is more easily absorbed and the ideal body temperature is obtained quickly. On the other hand, if there is a threat of overheating, the color changes quickly to light, almost shiny, tones that reflect some of the solar radiation.

Nearly invisible. The gray, beige, and brownish red basic colors and the contour-dissolving body markings of bearded dragons are excellent camouflage in a habitat where subdued red, brown, and grey shades dominate. If an enemy approaches, the dragon usually relies on its camouflage and remains motionless. Therefore, even those who are familiar with the native habitat of bearded dragons often have difficulties spotting bearded dragons.

Threatening defense. Only after the dragon has been discovered and then does not have a chance to flee, will it face the enemy and attempt to intimidate it. Its coloration changes to black, while it flattens its body substantially, faces the attacker, erects its "beard" (see page 9), and opens its mouth wide, all in a threatening manner. This way, the dragon appears larger and more defensible, and the now well-visible spiny armor has a significant effect on any attacker.

No Problem with Large Prey

The search for food in the arid regions of Australia is laborious. To survive, an animal cannot be choosy. Thus, bearded dragons feed on nearly anything the sparse environment has to offer.

Large mouth. The main components of the diet are insects and plants. However, bearded dragons can also handle other, smaller reptiles and even small

---

How to Recognize **Lizards**

THE MOST IMPORTANT CHARACTERISTICS

Bearded dragons are lizards from the animal Class Reptilia, which includes crocodiles and turtles. Together with snakes, they form the Order Squamata, or scaled reptiles. Typical characteristics of a lizard include:

LEGS	In some lizard groups, legs have become regressed, similar to snakes.
TAIL	The tail serves as rudder while running and may be used as a grasping tool while climbing, a weapon, and a storehouse for fat.
SCALES	The outer skin layer consists of keratin and is dead. It protects against injuries and prevents the loss of fluid.
MOLTING	The old skin sloughs off and is replaced by a new one.
COLD-BLOODED	All lizards are cold-blooded and unable to regulate body temperature independently (poikilothermic). In order to obtain the necessary body temperature, they have to pick up energy externally (e.g., in the form of solar radiation).
EGGS	Lizards lay eggs. Some scaled reptiles give birth to live young, but even then development takes place inside an egg shell, which breaks during the laying process (ovoviviparity = reproduction in which young develop from eggs retained within the mother's body but separated from it by egg membranes).

specimens of their own kind. Even rather large prey—half its own size—will fit into their giant mouths. That is a point well worth remembering when it comes to keeping bearded dragons in a terrarium.

Used to starving. Bearded dragons are fast and skilled hunters that rely on vision, not scent, to recognize their prey. Like most reptiles, they can survive drought and starvation periods. During the Australian winter, dragons may go into winter dormancy and become active again in spring, when there are insects and fresh green feed in abundance again.

Many enemies. In addition to the hostile arid regions of Australia, beardeds still need to be aware of a multitude of enemies. These include giant monitors, snakes, and birds of prey, and even large specimens of their own kind.

Bearded Dragons Are Solitary

In the wild, bearded dragons live alone and defend their territory aggressively—a behavior that is characterized by sparse food availability. When another bearded dragon (of equal size) enters the territory, there will immediately be fierce fighting. Only during the mating season in spring will bearded dragons look actively for a partner. A few weeks after copulation, the female buries its clutch of eggs at a damp location, but she does not engage in any form of brood care. Immediately upon hatching, the young look after themselves, and prove to be quite competent hunters already at an early age. As another adaptation to the environment they live in, bearded dragons grow very rapidly if food is abundantly available. They are almost fully grown and sexually mature after one year. Some *Pogona* species follow human settlements, so that bearded dragons can even be found in cities, not infrequently while basking in the sun on roads and fence posts.

Bearded dragons are superbly camouflaged in their natural habitat. Shown here is a common bearded dragon.

Bearded Dragons—At a Glance

BEARD With the aid of the hyoid bone apparatus, they can expand a spiny pouch under the jaw into a fan. This spiny throat resembles a beard, which has led to the common and scientific name (Greek *Pogon* = beard).

SPINES AND SCALES The *Pogona* species have robust, keeled, and partially spiny scales. Substantial spines are present especially around the head, the neck, and along the sides. The arrangement of spines and scales is the distinguishing characteristic of particular species.

MODE OF LIFE Bearded dragons are active during the day. They are extremely fast and skilled hunters. They feed on small animals as well as on plants.

The Most Important Types of Behavior

Bearded dragons are solitary animals, and so their behavior, for intimidation and defense against other bearded dragons as well as toward enemies, plays a central role in the lives of these reptiles.

Defense of the Territory

These solitary animals defend their own territory uncompromisingly. The territory owner watches over its territory usually from an elevated vantage point and underlines its territorial claims with conspicuous coloration of the body, an erect body posture, and the tip of the tail pointing upward.

Threat and Fighting Behavior

Bearded dragons defend themselves through body language. A dominating dragon signals its supremacy to another dragon with repeated, quick head nodding. If the other bearded dragon replies in the same manner, there will rarely be a fight: both reptiles encircle each other with a flattened body, an inflated beard, and the mouth open in a threatening manner and attempt to intimidate each other with whip-like tail lashing. If that is not successful, both fighters will bite each other (preferably into the neck spines), pressing the opponent to the ground. Serious injuries are rare in nature, but in a terrarium, where there are no escape means for the loser, there can quickly be serious injuries.

Warming Up

Bearded dragons are active during the day and regularly bask in their preferred sunny locations in order to warm up their bodies. During low habitat temperatures, the body operates on "small flame," and the reptiles are nearly defenseless. Like all lizards, they cannot perspire, only "pant" through an open mouth to cool off. To protect themselves against overheating, they withdraw into caves or other shaded places.

This *P. vitticeps* has no means of escape. It attempts to intimidate its opponents by increasing its size and erecting its beard.

Anatomy and Senses

Tail

The tail is roundish and slightly longer than the body. The tail stabilizes running movements, serves as support when sitting, and is used as a weapon in defense. Beyond that, it is also an important fat storage site.

Ears

The sense of hearing plays a subordinate role. The oval-shaped ear opening is easy to recognize; as in all lizards, an external ear is absent in bearded dragons.

EARDRUM (tympanic membrane): The thin membrane is located just inside the ear and is easy to see.

Mouth

The mouth, which is very large, can be opened wide, enabling the bearded dragon to swallow even large prey in one piece. Panting with an open mouth provides some cooling for the body.

TEETH The strong teeth are placed closely together. The front teeth can be replaced when lost.

Throat Pouch (Beard)

With the aid of the hyoid bone apparatus, bearded dragons are able to erect their spiny throat pouch completely. This ability is variably developed in different species and is a defensive means. Because of that, the head appears to be much larger and with that the bearded dragon seems far more intimidating and capable of defending itself.

Eye

The optical sense plays a central role. The eyes are located laterally on the head; the nictitating membrane has a protective function. Bearded dragons can recognize colors.
PARIETAL EYE The "third eye" on top of the head perceives light and darkness.

Skin

Thick and robust, skin prevents loss of fluid and protects against injuries and UV radiation.
SPINES Strong spines are located on the head, neck, and along the sides. They are used as a deterrent and for protection against predators.
COLORATION Changeable from light to dark for temperature compensation and during excitement.

Legs and Claws

LEGS Strong and muscular. They give these lizards rapid acceleration and high running speeds, however, only for a very short distance.
CLAWS Important for digging in hard soil and for climbing.

Will Bearded Dragons Suit Me?

Bearded dragons grow to a length of almost half a yard. They have special food requirements and live for about 10 years. Do not let the cute appearance of young beardeds and a favorable price tempt you into an impulse purchase.

Large Terrarium for Large Animals

Looking at a tiny, barely finger-long hatchling *Pogona vitticeps*, it is hard to imagine that within less than a year it will develop into a nearly 20-inch (50-cm) long lizard. As soon as the juveniles have outgrown the rearing terrarium, transfer them to a much larger container. *Pogona* species will only exhibit their fascinating behavior when they have sufficient space. Although they spend many hours basking motionless in the sun, bearded dragons can be very active. A pair of *Pogona vitticeps* requires a terrarium of at least 63 × 32 × 32 inches (160 × 80 × 80 cm); however, a terrarium of 79 × 32 × 32 inches (200 × 80 × 80 cm) will be better yet. For the smaller *Pogona henrylaw-*

Although keeping bearded dragons is not very expensive, it presupposes a detailed knowledge of the husbandry conditions that must be provided for these animals.

soni, one should plan for at least 47 × 24 × 24 inches (120 × 60 × 60 cm).

Partnership for Many Years

Bearded dragons have a life expectancy of more than 10 years. This needs to be taken into consideration before buying one. If, at some later stage, the dragons can no longer be kept, it is often difficult to find someone interested in adult bearded dragons. For accommodation reasons alone, it is virtually impossible to integrate adult bearded dragons into an established group of dragons.

Diet, Care, and Costs

Live food A large part of the diet consists of live insects such as crickets and related insect species (see page 46). Anyone who is revolted by these insects should not keep dragons. It must be anticipated that occasionally a food animal disappears in a corner somewhere, and then disturbs the night's sleep in your house or apartment, with loud chirping.
Costs *Pogona* species are exotic reptiles with specific requirements in terms of temperature and lighting conditions (see page 26). The financial investment for the basic equipment needed to keep bearded dragons (terrarium, furnishings, and technical components) and maintenance (electricity, food, possible veterinary costs) is not insignificant.
Vacation During the winter, vacation is not a problem if it falls into the dragon's dormancy period (see page 52). During the summer, they can be left alone for 3 to 4 days, since they get by without food for short periods. In fact, a fasting period is often good for bearded dragons since they are usually overfed in a terrarium. If you are out for an extended period, the bearded dragons will need to be looked after twice a week.

Stress-free **Transportation**

TIP FROM
DRAGON EXPERT
Manfred Au

TRAVEL AS SINGLE Bearded dragons must be packaged individually, so that they do not excite each other.

DARK CONTAINER Each lizard is placed into a plastic container large enough for the animal to move about inside. The container is placed inside a Styrofoam box so that the animal is protected against cold and heat and is in a dark environment. Here the lizard will quickly calm down again.

WATER For transport during the colder months, a warming flask or a drinking bottle with warm water should be provided. For the summer, there needs to be cold water in the Styrofoam box.

CAR TRANSPORT RISK Neither in the summer nor in the winter should reptiles be left unprotected in a motor vehicle. This could result in heatstroke or freezing to death, respectively.

DISPATCH BY MAIL It is permissible to ship lizards via U.S. mail. You cannot be guaranteed live delivery, because you cannot control the temperature of conditions the lizards will be subjected to.

DIRECT PICKUP When possible, always pick them up yourself. FedEx is a fast, dependable alternative.

Distribution and Description of Species

Bearded dragons are distributed throughout nearly the entire Australian continent. They are absent only from the wet tropical north, the southwest and southeast, and Tasmania. If the location is known where a particular specimen has been found, that in itself provides already a relatively safe species identification.

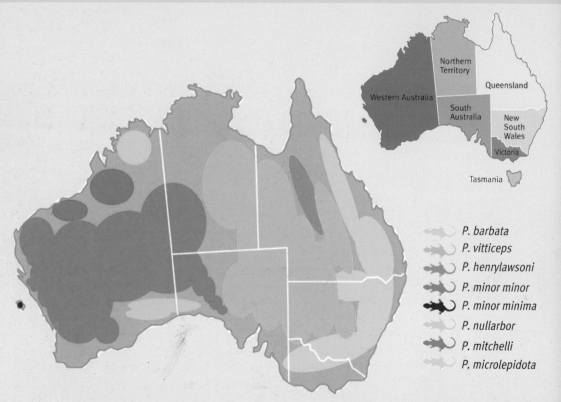

Northern Territory

Queensland

Western Australia

South Australia

New South Wales

Victoria

Tasmania

- P. barbata
- P. vitticeps
- P. henrylawsoni
- P. minor minor
- P. minor minima
- P. nullarbor
- P. mitchelli
- P. microlepidota

The genus *Pogona* includes seven species: *P. barbata, P. henrylawsoni, P. microlepidota, P. minor, P. mitchelli, P. nullabor, P. vitticeps*. Two subspecies have been described for *Pogona minor*: *P. minor minor* and *P. minor minima*.

Pogona vitticeps
Common Bearded Dragon

Distribution Central, western, and southern Queensland; central and eastern Northern Territory; central and western New South Wales; central, northern, and eastern South Australia. **Size** Head-body length up to 11 inches (27 cm), including tail up to 22 inches (55 cm), maximally 24 inches (60 cm). **Description** Large, broad, and compact, with very well-developed, spiny "beard"; strong spines on head, neck, and along sides. Variable coloration. There are brown, beige, yellow, and red *Pogona vitticeps*. Body markings are only weakly developed in adult specimens. The tail is short and strong, with a faint banded pattern. **Habitat** Dry interior of eastern Australia, predominantly in grass- and bush-land savannas, but also in open forests. **Terrarium maintenance** *P. vitticeps* is particularly well suited to captivity. These dragons will quickly become friendly, and they are less aggressive among themselves than the other species are.

Pogona henrylawsoni
Lawson's Bearded Dragon

Distribution Central and western Queensland. **Size** Head-body length 5 inches (13 cm), total length to about 12 inches (30 cm). **Description** Small, compact body with large head. Females larger than males. Beard barely developed; spines along greenish brown to beige colored back, sometimes specimens with reddish legs and sides. Frequently with spotted pattern on both sides of the vertebral column. Tail with banded pattern, normal or faint. **Habitat** Dry grassy and bush lands. Flees into ground burrows when in danger. **Terrarium maintenance** Second most commonly kept species; not quite as friendly as *Pogona vitticeps*. Since specimens are often incompatible with each other, they need to be kept (preferably) individually. In spite of the small body size, a large terrarium should be provided so that the dragons can avoid each other.

Pogona barbata
Eastern Bearded Dragon

Distribution Coastal areas of eastern Australia, along the southwest coast of South Australia and in central Victoria.
Size Head-to-body length more than 10 inches (25 cm), in total up to 24 inches (60 cm), rarely to 30 inches (75 cm).
Description Large and slender, beard and spines well developed. Gray back with light diamond-shaped markings along the vertebral column. Tip of tail and throat dark gray to black. Specimens from specific locations can have bright yellow head and flanks. Rarely kept in captivity.

Pogona nullarbor
Nullabor Bearded Dragon

Distribution Nullabor Plain in southeastern Western Australia and in southwestern South Australia.
Size Head-body length 6 inches (15 cm), in total more than 12 inches (30 cm). **Description** Rather spiny species with moderately developed beard. Back gray to reddish brown, sometimes rather contrastingly colored; bright cross bands. Tail strongly banded. Throat with 3 to 4 bright, irregularly shaped bands. This species is generally not kept in terrariums.

Pogona mitchelli
Mitchell's Bearded Dragon

Distribution Northwest coast of Western Australia.
Size Head-to body-length up to 7 inches (18 cm); in total up to 15 inches (37 cm). **Description** This species has a weakly developed beard without spines; however, there are some spines on head and neck and along the flanks. Back with beige to yellow-brown coloration; markings not particularly contrasting. This species is rarely ever kept in terrariums.

Pogona minor
Dwarf Bearded Dragon

Distribution Western, southwestern, and central Western Australia, southern South Australia. **Size** Head-body length 6 inches (15 cm), in total to 16 inches (40 cm). **Description** Medium-long spines and weakly developed beard without spiny scales. Back is gray-brown with beige-colored spots along the vertebral column. One dark spot each on the right and left shoulder. Not commonly kept. **Subspecies** The delineation of *P. minor minima* as a sub-species of the nominal form *P. minor* is still being debated.

Pogona vitticeps
Common Bearded Dragon

Color Variety Of all dragons, the common bearded dragon is the most commonly bred species in captivity. Occasionally, this has given rise to color morphs. This sub-adult specimen is uniformly dark and has dark eyes. Some smaller body parts are totally without darker pigments. The clutch, from where the specimen originates, contained several juveniles of the same color.

Pogona vitticeps
Common Bearded Dragon

Color Variety In recent years, dragon breeders have become involved increasingly in the production of new color varieties. There are now *Pogona vitticeps* in a multitude of remarkably beautiful colors. Some hobbyists will pay significant amounts of money for such—often still rather rare—color varieties. The specimen shown here has a red beard and enhanced red color pigments along its sides and back.

17

The Feel-Good Home

Keeping exotic animals from tropical regions successfully also means having to meet their specific requirements. That applies to accommodation and equipment, as well as to microclimate and diet. For bearded dragons, a species-specific habitat can only be established in a terrarium.

A Tailor-Made Home

All bearded dragon species are native to Australia (see Distribution and Description of Species, pages 14–17), and have become adapted—in terms of their body structure, physiology, and behavior—to a hot and dry environment.

Terrarium with a Large Footprint

Bearded dragons are primarily ground-dwelling lizards. With their flattened bodies, they are specifically equipped for this type of life. Although most species can climb very well, they usually remain in the lower parts of a tree and prefer the thick branches. Therefore, a terrarium suitable for dragons must have the largest possible floor area. The precise measurements are dependent on species and size of the dragons and the number of intended inhabitants of the terrarium.

Principally Dry and Warm

Bearded dragons will start feeling very comfortable with an ambient temperature of at least 77 to 82°F (25 to 28°C). Equally important is a very low humidity (40% during the day), adequate ventilation, and a brightly illuminated terrarium.

Safe Feeding

Bearded dragons feed principally on live insects, which they capture with a quick jump, following a brief stalking. Such prey is easily offered in a terrarium, where the insects cannot escape, and the hunting behavior of bearded dragons is easy to observe.

Mini-terrarium for the Progeny

A separate, small terrarium is required for rearing young bearded dragons. When young, they are still clumsy hunters and will not be able to capture sufficient food in a large terrarium.

Things to Watch For in a Terrarium

Selection of a particular size terrarium is dependent upon the species and number of animals you wish to keep in it. Other criteria apply to rearing young bearded dragons. Whether you are going to buy a prefabricated terrarium or build a domicile yourself, the terrarium must fulfill certain basic requirements. That includes a large floor area, sufficient lighting and effective ventilation, and different temperature zones. Set up the terrarium where the animals can be observed in comfort.

Bearded Dragons Require Fresh Air

A central point for dragon accommodation is effective ventilation. In order to ensure this, at least half of the cover of the terrarium needs to be made of wire mesh. Unfortunately, most commercial models only have a small ventilation screen, and so they are usually not suitable. The ideal solution would be a terrarium that is open at the top, but that, of course, is less than practical. In addition to ventilation in the terrarium cover, there need to be small air vents in the lower area of the container, in order to ensure fresh air circulation.

Glass or Wooden Terrarium?

Glass Nearly all commercially available terrariums are made of glass. Advantages: Optically appealing, easy to clean, and up to a length of about 60 inches (1.5 m), they are relatively cost-effective. Disadvantages: The risk of breakage can never be

The bearded dragon terrarium can be furnished very simply. The important thing is the largest possible floor area. Too many rocks and roots obstruct movement in the terrarium.

completely excluded, and a tank larger than 60 inches is very heavy and usually expensive.
Wood Suitable wooden terrariums for reptiles are rarely available. Advantages: Wood can be processed in a number of ways, and with little additional expenditure, it is easy to drill holes for cable leads, etc. Even large manufactured terrariums of this type are relatively lightweight and cost-effective. Disadvantages: Less attractive than glass containers; the terrarium occupants cannot be viewed unobstructed from every viewing angle.

Prefabricated or DIY Construction?

Prefabricated terrarium For commercially available glass terrariums up to a length of 60 inches (1.5 m), there is usually a large selection, mostly at moderate prices. Even rearing tanks with side length of 24 inches (60 cm) are distinctly cost-effective. Large terrariums, which are custom made, are significantly more expensive.
DIY construction Anyone making a terrarium according to his or her own specification can adapt it to particular requirements and fit it to the available space. However, building the terrarium yourself is really only cost-effective for large tanks.

Rearing and Treatment Tanks

Rearing tank Anyone wanting to breed these

dragons will need a separate terrarium to accommodate the young.
Treatment tank A small "treatment room" provides for the care of sick or injured animals. It must be completely furnished to meet all standard requirements of bearded dragons.

Correct Location

> Never in direct sunlight. Excessive solar radiation can lead to heat stroke. A cooler location is preferable to one that is warmer, because a terrarium is easier to heat than to cool down.
> In the middle of "family life." Place the terrarium at a location with an active (people) environment, approximately at table level. This way the dragons quickly adapt to your proximity.

Most bearded dragons, like this *P. mitchelli*, are very good climbers. Roots are popular vantage points.

Basic Equipment Needed

Bearded dragons do not have excessive demands in terms of accommodation. Apart from the substrate, rocks and roots can be used as decoration in a terrarium for bearded dragons.

Substrate

Here are several substrate possibilities:

> A cost effective and indeed acceptable solution is small-grained, washed gravel.

> Substrate made up of digestible calcium sand is new and relatively expensive. If it is swallowed, it supplies additional calcium.

> Even loamy red sand, called "digging clay" by some pet supply dealers, is suitable. It is placed moist into the tank and pressed against the bottom into desired landscape features. It hardens when it is dry. Dragons love this material and their claws are suitably worn down in due course.

> Fine sand is totally unsuitable. The grains stick to green feed and food animals, are inadvertently swallowed, and remain in the digestive tract and even cause intestinal blockage.

> Very young dragons are kept in a tank without loose substrate in order to avoid the danger of

A dragon cage does not need to be elaborate, but it does need to provide room, warmth, hiding and basking spaces, as well as space for food and water dishes.

intestinal blockage, in case the animals pick up substrate particles while feeding.

Rocks and Roots

Rocks and roots are the typical landscaping elements for a terrarium. Since bearded dragons are strong and like to dig, you must use only heavy rocks and roots. All objects must rest directly on the floor of the terrarium so that digging animals are not injured or killed by heavy collapsing landscape components. A flat, rocky tile, installed below the hot spot, quickly becomes a favorable resting place. Rock absorbs heat and the lizards can warm themselves from above and below. Climbing and hiding facilities are easily made from cork tubes.

Plants

Most plants are not suitable for a bearded dragon terrarium. They will be chewed on, flattened, or die from the dry heat. Moreover, many indoor plants are toxic for lizards. The only plants that can safely be used are succulents and agave, but the tips of the lower leaves should be rounded off with a knife or a pair of scissors. Plastic plants as decoration are not the worst choice that can be made.

Sight Barriers

The back of the terrarium and the sidewalls should be covered with some opaque adhesive material or, preferably, structured as rocky walls. The dragons feel more secure when they are covered all around except for the front glass. Commercially available back walls are a bit expensive; they are usually made out of Styrofoam and plaster.

Attractive and **Species-Correct Living**

TIPS FROM
DRAGON EXPERT
Manfred Au

SECOND FLOOR Increase the total floor area in the terrarium by installing a plaster-covered sheet of Styrofoam halfway up the height, as a so-called mezzanine floor, that extends along the entire length of the terrarium. Stability is provided by shelf angle brackets that are used to attach the sheet to the back wall. Access for the bearded dragons can be by means of a cork tube.

LESS IS MORE Limit yourself to a few wooden pieces and some rocks. A single type of rock, that matches the substrate and the back wall, especially with a decorative root in the center, often achieves the most natural appearance, as if they are in their natural habitat.

BRIGHT AND FRIENDLY Select bright colors for bottom and walls; dark tones absorb light.

PLANTS TO LOOK AT Anyone who wants to look at particularly attractive plants in the bearded terrarium can set up a second (plants only) terrarium directly behind the one with the dragons. The tank in the back can then be planted as desired and is given the appropriate plant climate. That tank then must also be illuminated.

The Bearded Dragon Terrarium

Back Wall

Back wall and side walls of the terrarium are covered with an adhesive plastic foil, or better yet with a rock wall made of plaster and tinted Styrofoam, in order to provide the dragons with additional climbing areas as well as sight barriers. A coat of water-based clear polyurethane (thoroughly dried) will protect the walls.

Second Floor

A sheet of Styrofoam installed half way up the back wall increases the overall floor space.

Climbing Branch

A ramp of cork oak is an ideal climbing aid for bearded dragons, to get from the main floor of the terrarium to the second (mezzanine) floor. At the same time, it is also an attractive decorative item.

Floor

The bottom substrate must not be too fine, and according to the number of inhabitants and size of the terrarium, it needs to be cleaned or replaced several times a year. A solid floor provides adequate wear for the claws of bearded dragons.

Ventilation

Fresh air enters via the ventilation slots and escapes through slots in the tank cover.

Terrarium Cover

At least half of the cover should consist of wire mesh, in order to ensure adequate air ventilation inside the terrarium.

Heat Lamps

Varied wattage heat lamps are suspended from the ceiling above respective basking sites. This way, the bearded dragon can select from several temperature zones.

Thermometer

The temperature can be monitored at any time by using several thermometers distributed throughout the terrarium.

Lighting

For standard-sized terrariums, the lighting and heat lamps should always be attached outside the container. Only for very tall and large terrariums can these elements also be installed inside the tank, since the occupants are not likely to come in to direct contact with them.

Sliding Glass Panels

Sand can fall onto the running tracks, which makes sliding the panels difficult or impossible. Regular vacuuming will keep the sand out and facilitate the smooth running of the panels.

Terrarium Technology

The bearded dragon terrarium requires very little technical support components. The only equipment needed for these relatively undemanding exotics are lighting and heating sources.

Lighting

Lighting, apart from temperature, plays a decisive role in the husbandry of reptiles. Both factors together determine the daily—and annual—rhythm of these animals. For instance, certain temperatures and amounts of light trigger reproductive behavior and the onset of winter dormancy. Bearded dragons come from a light-flooded environment and have become adapted to maximum brightness. Only under such conditions are bearded dragons contented. With appropriate lighting in the terrarium, one can attempt to simulate their natural environmental conditions. For bearded dragons it can never be too bright.

Fluorescent lights Fluorescent tubes are an ideal light source for the bearded dragon terrarium, since they provide a lot of light cheaply. Use those that promise full-spectrum lighting. They are available in different lengths, sizes, and light colors, and as special UV tubes. Recommendation: Use the substantially brighter T5 HO tubes instead of the older T8 tubes.

The tubes should cover the entire length of the terrarium, and always be operated in conjunction with a reflector that increases the brightness by almost 100%. Fluorescent tubes are particularly suited for small, long, and low terrariums. Two or three T5 tubes with a reflector represent the minimum required for adequate illumination of a tank with the dimensions 59 × 32 × 32 inches (150 × 80 × 80 cm). These tubes hardly give off any heat. In terms of purchase price

and operation, they are comparatively inexpensive.

Compact fluorescent The luminous efficiency of compact fluorescents is sufficiently high only over a small area and should be confined to very small terrariums, for instance a rearing or treatment tank.

Mercury vapor lamps (HQL) Self-ballasted mercury vapor lamps yield the best lighting for beardeds and must be operated with a ballast unit. The purchase price is moderate; however, energy consumption relative to luminous efficiency is high. These lamps are available in 50, 80, and 125 watts and are suitable for medium-high to high terrariums. They spotlight a small area; the light color is of medium quality. Advantages of these plans include a reduced UV radiation component and the emission of heat. When reptiles can select exposure to different heat sources, they usually prefer mercury vapor lamps. In the U.S. one good example is the T-Rex.

Combination set Two HQL lamps, each with 125 watts, and two to three fluorescent lamps are sufficient as light and heat sources for a terrarium that is 63 × 32× 32 inches (160 × 80 × 80 cm).

Metal vapor lamps These lamps provide extremely bright light, resembling daylight. They give off a lot of heat and are suitable only for high and well-ventilated terrariums. These lamps are expensive, and energy consumption is at a medium level.

UV-Lamps In terms of size, fluorescent tubes and lamps as UV sources are suitable for permanent operation in a bearded dragon terrarium. One UV economy lamp covers only a limited area. Bearded dragons can see under UV illumination. Without UV lighting the reptiles are missing out on this essential sensory area. In my experiences, UV light appears to

1 Fluorescent tubes should be replaced after at most 18 months in operation, since the light color changes and the luminous efficiency becomes distinctly less.

2 Compact household fluorescents are cost-effective light sources that hardly give off any heat. A disadvantage is that they may easily break.

3 All heat sources, used in conjunction with a terrarium, should have a protective screen, so that the reptiles cannot come into direct contact with them.

4 Heating mats can become brittle in time. They must be checked at regular intervals, in order to prevent the risk of electric shock.

have a positive effect on the well-being of bearded dragons. UV light is essential for the synthesis of vitamin D. For that particular purpose, however, you should use special lamps, such as T-Rex Active UV (at least three to four times per week, 30 minutes each), since normal UV lamps barely stimulate vitamin synthesis. Many reptile keepers use the T-Rex UV bulb daily as the heating-basking light.

Heat Sources

Heat lamps Most light sources also give off heat; only compact fluorescent and fluorescent tubes produce relatively cold light. The terrarium temperature should be 79 to 90°F (26 to 32°C) during the day, with sun bathing places of approximately 104°F (40°C), and cooler areas of 68 to 77°F (20 to 25°C), where there are no heat lamps installed. If it gets too hot inside the terrarium, the ventilation needs to be improved. Alternately (or in addition), warm air can be removed with a slow running exhaust fan. Excess

heat can lead to the demise of the reptiles, since they cannot reduce their body temperature through perspiration. During the night, all heat sources should be turned off. The temperature reduction promotes well-being and the health of the animals.

Spotlight Spotlights are suitable for heating small areas, such as sunbathing sites.

Floor heating The most natural warmth in a terrarium comes from above, preferably generated by heat lamps. However, it can also be helpful to supplement this heat regimen with floor heating. For that, a reptile heating mat is better suited than a heating cable. For a glass terrarium, the heating mat is placed on an insulating mat below the tank. This ensures that the heat is given off upward. In a wooden terrarium, the heating mat or heating cable is placed onto the floor of the tank. Since accidents cannot be avoided (when digging dragons encounter the heating source), it is better not to use floor heating in a wooden tank.

Important Accessories

Electric or electronic indicators, switches, and monitoring devices make it easier and safer to operate a terrarium and ensure the automatic control of the most important functions and devices.

Thermometer

You must have a thermometer when operating a bearded dragon terrarium.
> Digital. In glass terrariums, one normally uses digital, plastic thermometers that can be stuck to the walls.
> Indicator test. First, check the precision of the thermometer. Deviations of up to 18°F (10°C) are not uncommon.
> Remote sensor. Models with a remote sensor can be used in wooden terrariums. The temperature sensor can be introduced through a hole in the back wall of the tank, while the thermometer is attached to the outside, where it is easy to read.
> At a glance. Maximum-minimum thermometers are very practical for terrariums. Apart from the actual (current) temperature, they also show the highest and lowest value over the recording period. This way the nocturnal temperature drop is also easy to monitor.
> Glass thermometers. Never use glass thermometers. If the housing breaks, tiny glass splinters represent a great danger to the reptiles.
> Complete control. With several thermometers distributed throughout the terrarium, you have maximum control over the various climatic zones.

Thermostat

As soon as a preselected temperature is reached, the thermostat will turn off the attached equipment item. The automatic shutdown of heat sources can, for instance in summer, prevent any potential overheating.

Automatic Timers

The activities of reptiles on a daily or annual basis are controlled by light and temperature. With an automatic timer one can regulate the on and off periods during the day and simulate seasonal variations. Select an electronic timer with reserve that is able to bridge a power failure.

Dimmers

Dimmers control the operating output of equipment attached to it (e.g., heat lamps, heating mat) and will adjust variable requirements in response to different annual seasons. Some light sources cannot be dimmed, or they may require special modifications for that purpose. Solicit appropriate salesperson advice.

Caution: Electricity!

OFFICIAL TEST SEAL Electricity inside a terrarium is a potential source of danger. Use only electrical appliances that carry an official seal of approval.

SAFETY FIRST Remove faulty or damaged equipment immediately off-line.

PROFESSIONAL HELP Experts must always do repairs of electrical equipment and associated components.

REARING TANK The terrarium used for rearing young bearded dragons must fulfill the same technical requirements as a tank for mature *Pogona*. However, in terms of dimensions it should be significantly smaller, since young dragons are still unskilled hunters, and they will not be able to catch prey in a large terrarium. For safety reasons, one should do without any bottom substrate at all or use paper towels or perhaps calcium sand that can be eaten and digested without dangers.

QUARANTINE STATION The terrarium for the treatment of sick or injured dragons does not need to be very large. The furnishings for such a tank can be limited to the essential components. This then facilitates cleaning, which is particularly important for sick animals. Equipment required: heating and lighting source, water container, hiding opportunities. Instead of substrate, the bottom is covered only with paper toweling that must be changed daily.

TRANSPORT BOX A plastic terrarium with cover is ideal for transporting reptiles (e.g., to a veterinarian). Important: Inside of the container must be kept dark for extended transportation times.

Purchase and Maintenance

Bearded dragons are among the most popular exotic pets. They combine the originality of reptiles and the friendly behavior of pets. Apart from thoroughly informing yourself prior to the purchase, the selection of suitable specimens forms the basis for successfully keeping these animals.

When Lizards Come Into Your Home

Bearded dragons are relatively undemanding. However, like other pets, they too will bring some changes to your life; they require space, regular care, and attention.

Space Requirement

The terrarium for the bearded dragon must not be too small. The minimum floor space for a pair of *Pogona vitticeps* is 63 × 32 inches (160 × 80 cm), for two specimens of the smaller *P. henrylawsoni*, the minimum dimensions should be 47 × 24 inches (120 × 60 cm). When selecting the location of the terrarium, it is important to make sure that it will not be in direct sunlight, in order to avoid excessive heat inside the terrarium. Place the container in such a way that is easy for you to observe the animals. You should have a second, smaller tank ready, so that if an animal gets sick or injured, you can separate it for a while from the others, in order to give it special attention.

Feeding and Cleaning

Feeding Adult bearded dragons must be fed every 2 or 3 days, juveniles daily. Since *Pogona* feed principally on insects, it is advisable to keep an ample supply of such food organisms on hand.

Cleaning Replace the drinking water daily, and at the same time clean the water container. Also on a daily basis, you need to remove all excreta, which tend to smell very strongly.

Monitoring Check for possible unusual behavior among the animals, and monitor the temperature in the terrarium regularly.

Vacation During the summer vacation, your bearded dragons will need to be attended to every 3 to 4 days; during the colder period of the year, the animals go into winter dormancy.

Costs Apart from the initial acquisition costs, you also need to plan for ongoing expenses for live food and electricity for heating and lighting.

Selection and Purchase

Impulse purchases of bearded dragons are not uncommon. Many lizard fanciers are tempted by cheap offers or may be only insufficiently informed by an unscrupulous sales clerk about the real care requirements and follow-up costs. Lack of knowledge and experience is often the reason many of these reptiles either die during the first few weeks of their new ownership or will be given away. Prior to the purchase, it is important to resolve whether you can meet the basic prerequisites for keeping a pair of bearded dragons (see page 31).

Considerations Prior to the Purchase

Does everybody agree? Bearded dragons require regular care and attention. Proceed with the purchase only when all family members agree and recognize that the odd food animal will escape.

Bearded dragons must not be placed in the care of children. They are not playthings or cuddle toys.

Who is responsible? Taking care of the terrarium occupants must not become a random matter. It is of paramount importance that you determine beforehand who is responsible for the care of the animals, and who helps out if needed. Because of special maintenance requirements and the technical components in use around the terrarium, the responsibility must never be left to children.

Room for how many dragons? The decision for the species and number of specimens to be kept depends on the space available (i.e., whether there is room to set up a large terrarium or possibly two). The smaller *Pogona henrylawsoni* requires less space than *P. vitticeps*. It is only possible to keep a single male together with one or more females. The larger the group, the larger the terrarium has to be.

Progeny for bearded dragons? If you want to breed these reptiles, you need to plan for sufficient room for two animals. You can probably get a young pair from a breeder. An experienced breeder can recognize the sex of these dragons when they are a few months old and will offer you a suitable duo.

A lizard for beginners Anyone without prior experience in keeping reptiles should start out with a single dragon to avoid mistakes that occur when a pair is kept. After a few months a second animal of about the same size may be considered.

Emergency help Where can I get advice about care and maintenance problems? Where can I find a veterinarian with reptile experience? Who will look after my dragons when I am on vacation? You will need to resolve all of these questions before you proceed with the purchase. The first point of contact is usually the breeder or the pet shop

If the husbandry is satisfactory and there are appropriate habitat conditions in place, young bearded dragons tend to grow incredibly fast—2 inches (5 cm) or more a month! Pictured here is a juvenile specimen of the common bearded dragon (*Pogona vitticeps*).

owner, plus there are numerous pages dealing with bearded dragons on the Internet.

Important Purchase Considerations

The exportation of bearded dragons from Australia has been prohibited for many years now. All animals that are being held now are the progeny of many generations of captive breeding. Consequently, the differences in the quality of animals available are correspondingly large. The purchase

Online Sources for Information

Some states have wildlife licensing requirements and caging regulations for reptiles. There may be municipal guidelines as well. Check with your local Parks and Wildlife office before purchasing a reptile.

of such an animal is primarily a matter of trust, since external symptoms of any sort can only be seen in seriously ill or very poorly kept specimens. With that, early disease symptoms are easily overlooked. Beginners often have difficulties with a proper (quality) health assessment of dragons that they are about to purchase.

A reliable breeder Other terrarium hobbyists or even terrarium clubs are often willing to provide you with addresses of reputable breeders.

This is what to look for Do adult specimens as well as juveniles appear healthy and active? Are they accommodated in a species-correct manner? Does the terrarium convey a clean impression? Is the salesperson/breeder willing to provide you with detailed answers to your questions?

Option to purchase A reputable breeder or dealer will never knowingly sell you a sick bearded dragon. However, should the animal turn out to be sick, will he exchange it for a healthy one, or will he refund the purchase price?

Disease symptoms If there are the slightest doubts about the health of the bearded dragon, you should not proceed with the purchase. Here are some of the typical disease symptoms to look for: lame limbs; apathy; deformities of backbone, tail, or lower jaw; protruding pelvic bones; emaciated body and tail fins; open wounds; encrusted or closed eyes; bulging eyes ("google eyes" = exophthalmos); head resting on substrate; stumbling running movement; cramps. Never purchase an ill animal, even for humanitarian reasons.

Fecal sample Evidence of a possible infestation with parasites can be obtained from a fecal examination; however, this can only be done after the purchase.

This sub-adult *Pogona vitticeps* conveys an alert and healthy demeanor. The dragon checks out its surroundings in an alert manner.

How Expensive Is It to Keep Bearded Dragons?

CONSIDER YOUR EXPENDITURE Examine your household budget: keeping bearded dragons has two cost components: fixed costs and ongoing expenses for care and maintenance of, say, two adult common bearded dragons *(Pogona vitticeps)*.

FIXED COSTS Terrarium from $130 for material costs for home (DYI) construction, from $400 for an off-the-shelf model; heating and lighting, from $130; additional technical components (e.g., thermometer, automatic timer), $40; furnishings: substrate, roots, cork tubes and rocks, from $40.

RUNNING COSTS Live food $3.00 to $6.50 per week. Electricity 1.5 to 2.0 kilowatts per hour per day.

Moving Into the Terrarium

Before bearded dragons can move in, their new "home" needs to be completely furnished and fully functional. A trial run over a 48-hour period will tell you whether the terrarium climate conforms to the requirements of the future occupants.

Introducing and Conditioning

All bearded dragons that have been purchased must be introduced into the terrarium at the same time. This way you avoid territory issues where dragons that are added later on will be considered intruders and subsequently attacked. These reptiles adapt very readily to their new surroundings, and usually display their natural behavior within a few hours after arrival. Do not place more than one male to a cage.

These Are the Things You Must Watch for Now

Conspicuous changes of behavior during the first few days are always warning signals.

› Are all animals behaving normally and without recognizable limitations?

› Are they moving freely throughout the entire terrarium or do they attempt to hide?

› Do they accept food when it is offered?

› Are there no obvious digestive problems?

› Is one animal suppressed by the other occupants, so that it cannot feed properly, and is it always chased away from sunbathing sites?

The quarantine terrarium should be set up with basic equipment only, so that it is easy to clean and has only a few, well-controlled hiding places.

› Are the bearded dragons getting along well with each other or is there any serious aggression?

Sight barriers Install the terrarium decorations in such a manner that an intimidated, frightened animal can withdraw out of sight from the other terrarium occupants. This must include a sight protected sunbathing place. If such arrangement does not produce a satisfactory result, the suppressed animal needs to be removed from the terrarium.

Prey Under no circumstances should you keep bearded dragons of different sizes together in the same terrarium: the large ones will consider the small ones as prey.

The Be-All and End-All of Species-Correct Care

Although species-correct care of bearded dragons requires a certain flair, it does not present insurmountable problems for beginning terrarium hobbyists. Anyone who observes and complies with the important points will enjoy healthy and active animals for many years to come.

Solo or in a Group?

Keeping a single bearded dragon In their natural habitat, all bearded dragons are solitary and will look for a partner only during the breeding season. Other than that, they will avoid the proximity of other bearded dragons. Having said that, keeping only a single animal in a terrarium is indeed species-correct.

In a group If you want more activity in your reptile domicile, keep several bearded dragons together. This applies only to the less aggressive species, such as *Pogona vitticeps* and *P. henrylawsoni*. Both are suitable for beginners, but the remaining species should be kept only by experienced terrarium hobby-

These two babies enjoy jointly the warmth from a heat lamp. It takes a lot of experience to determine the sex of bearded dragons at this age.

ists. Such a group of bearded dragons can consist of several females, but only a single male.

Terrarium size The terrarium should have the following minimum dimensions: for an adult pair of *P. vitticeps* 63 × 32 × 32 inches (160 × 80 × 80 cm), for two adult *P. henrylawsoni* 47 × 24 × 24 inches (120 × 60 × 60 cm). Minimum size of a rearing tank for two to three juveniles: 24 × 12 × 12 inches (60 × 30 × 30 cm).

Group size The number of animals depends on the floor area of the terrarium. However, even in a large tank there is always only room for a single male; otherwise, there will be severe aggression between two males.

Age and size Make sure that your terrarium inhabitants are as close as possible in size. Small specimens are often considered as prey by large ones, even their own progeny. Bearded dragons can swallow surprisingly large prey.

Separate accommodation Bearded dragons that seem to be constantly suppressed by other occupants of the terrarium should be removed. Similarly, if the male pursues a gravid female too aggressively, it too should be removed until after the eggs have been laid. Similarly, separate sick and injured dragons.

Keeping Several Species Together

With other bearded dragons In principle, different bearded dragon species can be kept together in a terrarium; however, these can only be groups of females consisting of equal-size animals.

With other lizards Bearded dragons can also be kept together with other lizards, provided the terrarium occupants can all tolerate the same climatic conditions and are sufficiently large so that they are not considered as food by the bearded dragons. Suitable co-inhabitants can be frilled (or frill-neck) lizards

---

Gaining Trust Made Easy

TIPS FROM
DRAGON EXPERT
Manfred Au

CALM AND GENTLE Avoid hectic movements, and give the animal sufficient time to adjust to your proximity. Some will become friendly, while others will always keep their distance.

NEVER FROM ABOVE You can pick up a bearded dragon from the front or from the side, but never from above. Any approach from above is perceived as an attacking predator.

GENTLE HANDLING Never restrain a dragon against its will. When the animal tries to free itself, there can be injuries.

HAND FEEDING Tasty treats should be offered by hand, and let the dragons climb onto your open hand. Dragons perceive our body heat as pleasant.

NO, DRAGONS ARE NOT A TOY Contact between children and bearded dragons should occur only under supervision.

LEARNING THE BEHAVIOR When a bearded dragon closes its eyes and flattens its body, the animal is not feeling well or is scared. If it scratches on the front glass, it wants to be taken out of the terrarium.

(*Chlamydosaurus* sp.) and spiny-tailed lizards (*Uromastyx* sp.).

Climatic Conditions and Lighting

Temperature Bearded dragons prefer a dry and warm environment; therefore, it is vital to offer a temperature gradient in the terrarium: from 73 to 77°F (23 to 25°C) in the coolest zone, up to 86 to 91°F (30 to 33°C) in the warmest. The temperatures can even reach 104 to 113°F (40 to 45°C) over the sunbathing sites. The terrarium inhabitants can select their own feel-good area. At night, switch off heat sources.

Humidity The relative humidity inside the terrarium during the day should be about 40%, at night approximately 50%. If the humidity is too high, bearded dragons can get diseases, especially fungal infections.

Lighting Adjust the light cycle so that a day for the dragons during the summer months lasts 12 to 13 hours, in spring and autumn approximately 10 hours, and during winter dormancy lighting can be switched off completely. UV light is important for their health and well-being (see page 26), so expose them as often as possible to natural sunlight.

Winter Dormancy

During the winter months, bearded dragons enter a rest period (winter dormancy) for 2 to 3 months (see page 52), when their metabolism is significantly reduced. The ambient temperature should be about 64°F (18°C); heating and lighting remain turned off.

Feeding

The diet of bearded dragons consists of approximately two thirds animal matter (primarily live insects) and about one third vegetable matter, such as lettuce and fruit (see page 46). Adult specimens are fed only every second or third day; babies, three to six times a day determined by their appetite.

Quarantine

Before a new arrival is integrated within an existing group, it needs to be kept in a separate terrarium for several weeks (see page 29). Here you can readily check whether the animal is healthy and is not likely to infect other animals in the group with a disease.

Providing Holiday Care

Adult bearded dragons can do without food for several days, and so a brief vacation of a week does not represent any problems. Lowering the terrarium temperature reduces the metabolic rate. In the event of a longer absence, however, adult bearded dragons will need to be fed every 3 days; juveniles must be fed daily. If you take a vacation during the winter, you may wish to make plans so that it falls into the winter dormancy period of your bearded dragons.

A UV lamp, like this OSRAM UltraVitalux can be hard-wired into very large terrariums. In this photograph, the UV lamp is suspended out of reach of the bearded dragons.

Doing Everything Correctly Right from the Start

With a terrarium that offers sufficient room for bearded dragons, is sparingly yet interestingly decorated, and provides different climatic zones, you are laying the foundation for species-correct, successful maintenance of these reptiles.

What to do

What not to do

(+) If you do not have any experience with reptiles, start out as a terrarium hobbyist with a single dragon.

(+) Before the bearded dragons can move in, the terrarium must be completely set up and be fully functional.

(+) The microclimate in the terrarium is the single-most important factor for keeping bearded dragons successfully. Check the terrarium temperature daily.

(+) Provide your bearded dragons with quality, uncontaminated food. It is best to feed less rather than too much.

(+) Communicate regularly with other bearded dragon owners.

 Do not purchase bearded dragons that are sick or display conspicuous behavior abnormalities. Keeping and caring for such sick animals will very much exceed the abilities of beginners.

 Brightness and light play a central role in the life of dragons. Inadequate lighting and poor light quality increase susceptibilities to diseases.

(−) Bearded dragons are not playthings or cuddle toys. Their care must not be left to children.

 Terrariums with inadequate ventilation and air vents that are too narrow are not suited for keeping bearded dragons.

Breeding Bearded Dragons

Even for beginners, breeding *Pogona vitticeps* and *P. henrylawsoni* hardly ever presents any problems. By comparison, the other bearded dragon species are far more difficult to breed—one of the reasons why these are rarely available.

Sex Differences

At first sight, it is very difficult to distinguish between male and female bearded dragons. Males are characterized by pockets at the base of the tail behind the cloaca, the location of the so-called hemipenes, (i.e., paired copulating organs). Fully grown males can also be recognized by the presence of glands along the lower thighs of their hind legs, the femoral pores (see page 42).

Prerequisites for Breeding

Healthy, breeding females If a sick or weak female is used for breeding, there can be problems during the pregnancy. Under such conditions, it is not uncommon for egg binding to occur (see page 56), which can lead to the demise of the female unless treated in time.

Free of hereditary damages Weak constitutions and deformities are often genetically linked. If such animals are used for breeding, these defects are passed on to the next generation.

Not with young animals Females ready for breeding are those that have reached at least four fifths of their ultimate, adult size. Early breeding places an enormous physiological load on the body. Since growth in these lizards varies, it is not the age that is decisive for reproductive suitability and success, but solely the body size.

Suitable season The best time for breeding bearded dragons is during the first few weeks after completion of the winter dormancy. Rising temperatures and increasing daylight periods in the terrarium will trigger the courtship and mating drive and synchronize the behavior of male and female.

Bearded dragons communicate by means of gestures and colors. This female placates the male by "waving" with her arm, called circumduction.

This attractively marked *Pogona vitticeps* is still young. Unfortunately, the appealing coloration is often lost with maturity.

This young *P. henrylawsoni* is maintained on limestone pebble substrate. If some of the limestone particles are eaten, they can be completely digested.

Courtship and Mating

Within 3 weeks after the winter dormancy, the lighting period and temperatures in the terrarium should be adjusted in two or three stages to summer conditions.

› Usually it takes only a few days until the male commences courting the female with head nodding and with an erected beard that has turned jet black.

› At the start of the courtship the female still flees from the courting male and attempts to placate him with "arm waving."

› A few days later, often during the late morning hours, the female will then be ready for mating. She no longer runs away from the male, but instead signals her agreement with push-up like movements of her upper torso.

› During copulation the male generally bites into the neck of the female, twists his tail around hers, and inserts one of the two hemipenes into the cloaca. Copulation lasts about 30 seconds to 2 minutes.

› Once a bearded dragon female has mated, she can produce several successive clutches. However, in this form of cloacal sperm storage, the number of fertilized eggs will decrease in subsequent clutches.

› Watch the behavior of your dragons closely: if the female remains unwilling to mate for several days, she should be removed from the terrarium, otherwise she could be injured by the aggressively courting male.

› During the subsequent period, the female's appetite will increase and the animal will become distinctly heavier. During this phase a lot of quality, calorie-rich food must be offered. Occasionally, this can also include a prekilled pinkie.

› A sufficient supply of minerals and vitamins is also important for the nutrition of the gravid female (e.g., with Reptomin, or similar product available from your pet store). If this is inadequate, there can be problems when the eggs are laid (egg binding!).

Incubation and Rearing

The "pregnancy" (gravid condition) generally lasts 4 to 6 weeks. If, after that time, the female is not making any efforts to deposit her eggs in spite of the fact that there are suitable sites available, it can be an indication of egg binding. Rush the animal to a veterinarian.

Ideal Egg-laying Site

The female will dig at various sites in the terrarium until she finally finds a suitable place to deposit her eggs. At that point—at the latest—the male must be removed from the terrarium so as not to inter-

1 Femoral pores are only visible in adult males (see page 40). These glands are probably used for marking the territory.

2 In female bearded dragons, the femoral pores, located at the origin of the tail, are barely developed. These photos show the common bearded dragon.

fere with the egg-laying process. The ideal medium for egg laying is a slightly damp layer of sand, at least 8 inches (20 cm) thick. The female will dig to the bottom of the sand, deposit her eggs, and cover up the burrow meticulously.

Incubating the Eggs

Digging up the eggs Now the time has come for you to be actively involved, and dig up the eggs again. In *Pogona vitticeps* there are usually 20 to 30 eggs. Make sure that you do not damage the delicate eggs. During their developmental stage, the eggs can still be rotated, but after that they must no longer be moved. Any sand attached can be removed with a (soft) brush.

The correct incubating box Small Tupperware boxes are ideal for incubating the eggs, as are plastic shoe boxes. Since the air supply in such a box is totally adequate for the development of eggs, there is no need to provide additional ventilation holes. Advantage: the humidity inside the box remains more or less constant. You do not need to add water and thus avoid possible mistakes.

The correct substrate The incubating box is filled halfway with vermiculite or perlite (available from pet shops) as incubating substrate. Moisten the incubating substrate slightly; ideal is a weight ratio of 1:0.8 to 1:1 between substrate and water. Bury the eggs so that about one third of each egg protrudes above the substrate. Since the eggs will absorb a lot of moisture during the following weeks and increase their volume, place them at intervals of at least an inch (2 cm), side-by-side, in the medium of the incubating box.

Lots of warmth Place the incubating box at a location that has day temperatures of 79 to 84°F (26 to 29°C) and that must not fall below 68°F (20°C) at night. Commercially made incubating boxes for reptiles are available in several models from pet stores.

Hatching of the young Depending upon the temperature, bearded dragon progeny hatches in 50 to 70 days. Imminent hatching is usually indicated about 24 hours earlier, with the formation of "perspiration" in the form of droplets scattered over the surface of the eggs. Often the eggs will collapse prior to hatching. Young bearded dragons will cut the eggshell open with the aid of their egg tooth, which is a small, sharp thorn on the tip of the nose. It is shed shortly after hatching.

Rearing Bearded Dragons

› From their first day in life, newly hatched bearded dragons are totally independent. Therefore, raising them does not present major problems.

› To help the still clumsy youngsters catch prey, they should be reared in a small container, with approximate dimensions of 24 × 12 × 12 inches (60 × 30 × 30 cm), fitted out in a very simple manner so that food animals are unable to hide.

› During the first few weeks, there should not be any substrate at the bottom of the container; otherwise, the young dragons will inadvertently "eat" a lot of that while feeding.

› The young lizards will start feeding within the first 24 hours. Since they grow very rapidly, they require a quality diet (small insects and leafy greens, and fruit cut into small pieces that are easily swallowed). Important: For every second feeding, you should dust the food organisms with a calcium-vitamin mixture.

› When rearing several youngsters together, food

3 The female is digging a deep burrow to deposit her eggs. It is not uncommon for the female to dig at several sites before she selects a particular cave.

4 This juvenile bearded dragon, seen here inside the incubator, is 24 hours old. The empty eggshells indicate that its siblings have already hatched several days ago.

5 Young dragons are totally independent from their first day in life and display all the behaviors seen in adults, like here basking in the sun.

must be available around the clock; otherwise they will bite each other's legs and tails.

› It is advisable to provide a bath with lukewarm water, sufficiently shallow so that the animals can easily stand up in the water. Duration: Every second day for about 15 minutes.

› UV radiation (e.g., UltraVitalux or similar brand; distance from lamp to animals: 1 m) promotes development and fortifies the body system. Duration: Every second day for 30 minutes.

Fit and Healthy

By adhering to a species-correct diversified diet, maintaining a proper feeding strategy, and maintaining natural rest phases in conjunction with prophylactic health care, you are creating the best possible conditions for keeping your bearded dragons healthy and active for many years.

Diet Plan and Health Check

Although bearded dragons are not difficult to feed, you should stick to a few feeding rules. In matters of health, it is of vital importance to these lizards—more so than for any other pet—for you to keep in mind that the earlier a disease is recognized, the greater the chances of a successful treatment are.

Feeding Correctly

› In their inhospitable native country, bearded dragons must be satisfied with sparse food offering, and therefore these reptiles are not choosy. They accept insects, small reptiles, and small mammals as well as plant (green) food. Consequently, it is easy to provide a balanced diet and a lot of diversity within a comprehensive diet plan.

› Hunger periods of several days are no rarity in the wild. Even in the terrarium, you should not feed your bearded dragons every day. Of particular sig-

nificance is live food. When hunting and capturing prey, lizards can display their inherited behavior patterns and at the same time remain physically fit.

› Bearded dragons can do without water for a long period, but if given the opportunity, they like to drink or even take a bath. Therefore, fresh water should always be available in the terrarium.

Early Recognition of Diseases

› Behavioral disturbances and disease symptoms must always be taken seriously. If in doubt, always consult a veterinarian who has reptile experience, immediately.

› During the Australian winter, bearded dragons go into a two-month dormancy period. Even in a terrarium, such a rest period has a positive effect on the health of these animals; it will essentially extend their longevity.

Fundamentals of Nutrition

In the wild, bearded dragons feed primarily on animals such as insects, spiders, small mammals, and reptiles, and to a lesser degree on leaves, flowers, and fruits.

Mainly Live Food

All *Pogona* species lie in wait for their prey, preferably on some elevated vantage point. With a sudden leap, they overpower suitable prey that comes into their field of vision. It is not uncommon for such prey to be a small bearded dragon.

1 Crickets are generally offered for sale in boxes like these. At home, you need to transfer the food animals into larger containers for longer-term keeping.

2 Crickets are dusted with a vitamin-mineral powder and are then fed immediately so that they cannot clean themselves and wipe off the powder.

For juveniles In nature, growing bearded dragons feed exclusively on a protein-rich, animal diet. Therefore, when raising them in a terrarium, insects are the principal item on their beginning diet plan. However, it is very important to adapt small dragons early on to plant (green) food, so that they will accept such food later in their life.

More green feed for adults In the wild, the component of plant food eaten by young bearded dragons is approximately 30%, that of adults up to 50%. When rearing dragons in a terrarium, they should always receive a gradually increasing amount of plant food.

Suitable food animals Crickets (various species) and cockroaches are available throughout the year from specialist pet shops or mail order suppliers. These animals are best accommodated in a tall plastic terrarium with a lid, at a temperature of approximately 68°F (20°C). Prior to feeding them to bearded dragons, the food animals should be given a diet of fruit, oatmeal, carrots, and some dried fish food, for about 2 to 3 days. This is to provide the bearded dragons with sufficient vitamins. The fruit provides sufficient liquid for the food animals.

Breeding your own food animals Experienced terrarium keepers often breed their own food animals. This may not be more cost-effective (than purchasing them from a pet shop), but it does provide operational independence and better quality control over the food for your bearded dragons.

Fattening foods Mealworms and *Zophobas* ("superworms") are very fatty and should only be fed sparingly—if at all. These are kept simply in open boxes.

Plant Food (Green Feed)

The search for suitable green feed for bearded dragons is not difficult. During the warmer seasons of the year, you can find a variety of plants—such as leaves and flowers of dandelions, clover, daisies, and chickweed—on meadows and other grassy patches, which are eagerly taken by bearded dragons. During the winter months, you can offer leafy greens, pealed bell peppers, and carrots. All types of fruit can be offered throughout the year. The diverse offering of green feed guarantees a balanced and healthy food supply to your terrarium occupants.

Only food without chemicals! Prior to collecting green feed, make sure that the area where you are collecting has not been sprayed or otherwise chemically treated so that you do not run the risk of feeding toxins to your pets.

Food Alternatives

Small animals During the summer, inhabitants from meadows and other grassy areas provide a healthy and diverse alternative. Here too you need to make sure that the area has not been sprayed with chemicals.

Please note The meadow fauna also includes protected invertebrate animals that must not be collected (e.g., butterflies).

Young mice Mice that are still hairless (i.e., *pinkies*), can provide many important nutrients; therefore, they are a quality food for gravid females. For reasons of animal welfare, they can only be offered dead as food for bearded dragons.

Vitamins and Minerals

With various vitamin and mineral preparations, you can prevent nutritional deficiencies that can occur when reptiles are kept in a terrarium. Here, a central role is played by calcium and vitamin D3. An undersupply of these active ingredients can lead—especially in juveniles—to abnormal development of the bone and muscle skeleton. All food animals should be dusted with the appropriate supplement just prior to feeding them to bearded dragons. An additional calcium source can be small pieces of cuttlefish bone placed along the bottom of the terrarium. **To be kept refrigerated!** Vitamins are heat- and light-sensitive and must be stored in a cool, dark location.

Fluid Requirement

Although bearded dragons are native to an extremely dry environment, they like to drink often.

3 Yellow flowers, such as dandelion flowers, which are very healthy, are eaten keenly and are therefore often deliberately picked out by the dragons.

4 A mixed lettuce plate is a welcome diversity and a very vitamin-rich food offering, keenly accepted by the dragons.

Therefore, a shallow bowl with fresh water should be placed in every terrarium. Yet, since not all animals can be adapted to accept the drinking bowl, the interior of the terrarium should be sprayed with water daily with a flower atomizer, so that the inhabitants can lick the water droplets. When doing that, make sure that you avoid excessive wetness in the terrarium. In a permanently moist terrarium, there is an increased risk of infection to bearded dragons.

Enjoying a bath Some bearded dragons enjoy taking a warm bath. For that, the bowl should be filled so that the lizards can keep their legs firmly on the bottom without being completely submersed, at a water temperature of 86°F (30°C).

Feeding Rules

How often do I have to feed? Juveniles should be fed at least on a daily basis, and two thirds of the diet should consist of live food. Before feeding, all food animals need to be dusted with a vitamin-mineral mixture. Adults are given animal and plant food alternately, fasting every third day.

Avoid **Feeding Mistakes**

FEED SPARINGLY Adult bearded dragons should be fed rather less than more; otherwise, they become fat and complacent.

DO NOT FEED MEAT! Pork and beef are taboo. They are difficult to digest and can make the lizards sick.

POISON IN GREEN FEED Plants that are unfamiliar could be poisonous: do not feed or use these plants for decorating a terrarium.

When to feed? Early in the day is the best time to feed: the animals are sufficiently warmed up to succeed with prey capture and still have the remaining day for hunting and digesting.

Making fit Crickets and similarly active food animals are not easy to catch, even for fast-reacting bearded dragons. They provide diversity and keep the terrarium occupants fit.

Special Diets

Vitamins for sick dragons Sick and weakened bearded dragons must be fed daily, kept in a separate terrarium where they can be watched to make sure they eat properly. For full recovery, they need a vitamin-rich diet frequently supplemented with additional vitamin drops. Comply with dosage recommendations: an excessive supply is as dangerous as a deficiency.

Calories for gravid females The development of eggs places the females under considerable physical and physiological strain. In order to satisfy its extraordinary high food requirement, she should receive a daily diet of calorie and vitamin-rich food. At intervals of 4 to 5 days, she can be given a prekilled pinkie. Small pieces of cuttlefish bone in the diet provide the essential calcium.

After egg deposition Laying the eggs will require the last energy reserves from the female and weaken her body system substantially. So that the maternal animal regains its strength as quickly as possible, the daily feeding with calorie-rich food should be maintained for some time.

The bearded dragon species *Pogona mitchelli* is rarely ever found in a terrarium. These rather attractive, but solitary animals are occasionally rather aggressive among themselves.

Regular Maintenance Tasks

Regular care keeps your bearded dragons healthy and fit. These animals are relatively undemanding and require very little special care, and so it is even more important to execute the essential maintenance measures carefully and deliberately.

Remove Excretory Products

Bearded dragons are relatively large animals with an active metabolism that produces a lot of fecal matter, which smells less than pleasant. The excretory products consist of dark feces and a light-colored—solid—urine. To remove these items it is best to use a special fecal shovel or a plastic spoon. Since the animals keep running over their own fecal matter and so distribute it throughout the terrarium, the terrarium will become dirty relatively quickly. Therefore, regular cleaning is unavoidable. The substrate of the terrarium should be renewed completely once or twice a year. The timing for this is usually indicated by the developing, rather unpleasant odor.

After spraying the terrarium with the spray bottle, bearded dragons will lick the water drops with considerable perseverance. Some animals will take liquid only from such a source.

Bearded Dragons Like to Bathe

Although bearded dragons come from a rather arid environment, they also like to take a bath. You should provide them with this creature comfort on a regular basis. Moreover, it is really the only way to remove the dried-on dirt from the excrement scattered through the terrarium. The small plastic terrarium can be used as a bath container; if need be a hand washing basin will also suffice. With young dragons, you must make sure that the water level is not too high. When the animals can no longer stand in the water without going under, they often panic. Initially, juvenile dragons should be bathed individually. Later on, after they have become used to the procedure, all of them can get into the water together. However, they must still be monitored closely. Even in shallow water one of the animals can drown if another one climbs on top of it. A water temperature of about 86°F (30°C) is perceived as being very pleasant. At that temperature, the animals can remain in the bath for 10 to 15 minutes.

Dusting the Food Animals

Prior to being fed to the dragons, live food animals are placed into a plastic box or into an empty cricket can. Then, some vitamin-mineral powder is added to the container, the lid is closed and the container is gently shaken until all food animals are covered with powder. Immediately thereafter, they must be fed to the bearded dragons. This way it is avoided that the food animals rid themselves of powder. Discard the powder left in the container, and use fresh powder for every feeding. Older powder no longer sticks properly, and the sensitive vitamins often lose their effectiveness within 24 hours.

The Most Important **Feeding Rules**

TIPS FROM
DRAGON EXPERT
Manfred Au

ALL AT ONCE Crickets and other live food animals should be placed in the terrarium all at once. Not only will this feeding method permit weaker bearded dragons to catch food, but the food animals fleeing into all directions in the terrarium is a potent stimulus for the dragons.

EATING ALONE When weakened or submissive bearded dragons cannot catch sufficient food, they must be fed separately.

MEAT IS TABOO Meat does not contain sufficient roughage; therefore, it should not be fed to bearded dragons. This also includes beef heart.

VITAMINS The quality of food animals available is often rather variable. Therefore, before these are given to bearded dragons, the food animals must be fed a diet of vitamin-rich food for 3 to 4 days prior to being offered to the terrarium inhabitants.

MICE A gravid bearded dragon female can occasionally be given a prekilled pinkie.

LIVE FOOD Make sure you obtain quality live food animals. Animals from inferior breeding productions can introduce transmissible diseases.

Winter Dormancy

In their original habitat, all *Pogona* species go through a dormant period during the cooler time of the year. In Australia, this falls into the period from May through August. At that time, the day and night temperatures are lower, and food becomes scarce. Bearded dragons sleep through these months in burrows. All metabolic functions are lowered to "economy," energy consumption is greatly reduced, and although the animals do not feed, they barely lose any weight. Low temperatures and shorter daylight periods trigger winter dormancy.

Winter Dormancy in the Terrarium

The annual rhythm of winter dormancy is solidly anchored in the behavior pattern of bearded dragons. All dragons kept in captivity are the result of captive breeding, since there is a total ban on exporting wild bearded dragons out of Australia. This has been in effect for several decades already. In spite of such a long period without "new blood and fresh genetic material," bearded dragons in captivity now still withdraw to some quiet hiding place during the winter, even when the temperatures and lighting period in our terrariums remain unchanged.

Do Bearded Dragons Need a Rest Period?

During the inactive phase in the winter, the body system of bearded dragons rests and so, in effect, recharges its batteries. In essence then, the winter pause ensures that the animals remain fit for longer, which generally also extends their longevity. In addition, it synchronizes the reproductive activities of males and females, and triggers reproductive behavior after the winter dormancy period.

Preparations

In November or early December, or at the latest when the bearded dragons become noticeably quieter and less active, the necessary preparations should be made for the onset of winter dormancy:

When bathing, the dragons must be able to keep their legs securely on the floor of the bath container; otherwise, they will quickly panic.

1 BEFORE THE WINTER DORMANCY This *Pogona vitticeps* conveys an all-around healthy appearance and will be able to withstand the dormancy period without any problems.

2 REMAIN AWAKE Juveniles up to an age of 12 months should not have a winter dormancy period because they have not yet acquired sufficient body reserves.

3 TRAVEL CONTAINER Dragons can be transported in plastic aquariums that are placed inside a dark Styrofoam box.

Temperature and light You should lower the terrarium temperature gradually to about 64°F (18°C) over a period of 3 weeks. At the same time, reduce the daily lighting period to 7 or 8 hours. Later on, the light can be turned off completely. When the ambient temperatures are too high, bearded dragons will awaken from dormancy. That is a sign that their metabolism is too active and that too much energy is being used. Under these conditions, the animals will lose weight.

Duration The winter dormancy should last 2 months; however, 3 months would be better.

Resting sites Bearded dragons will look for resting sites they deem to be suitable. These can be caves and other hiding places; sometimes the reptiles select thick branches. If the temperature in the indoor terrarium is too high, the animals should be transferred to a cooler room. For that, a small terrarium can be used.

Spring awakening Once spring arrives, you will need to act in reverse by increasing the lighting period and temperature gradually, over about 3 weeks, back to normal levels.

Resting Period Is a Fasting Period

During the winter rest, the stomach of the bearded dragon needs to be completely empty. To achieve that, start to reduce the amount of food given at the same time that the temperature reduction regimen is begun. One week before the onset of the actual winter dormancy period, all feeding stops. Food remnants left in the stomach cannot be digested at low temperatures; any undigested food will injure the dragons. Drinking water must always be accessible to the reptiles, even during the rest period.

No Winter Rest

› Very young bearded dragons must be exempted from the winter dormancy, since their bodies do not yet have sufficient reserves to sustain them. Similarly, all dragons younger than 12 months can also be maintained without a rest period, and so they will grow faster.

› Sick or injured dragons must not be sent into winter dormancy either, since they will not be able to survive this phase. A fecal examination in autumn will inform you of a possible parasite infestation.

This Will Keep Your Animals Healthy

Bearded dragons are distinctly robust animals. Species-correct maintenance meets the demands of the animals in terms of terrarium climate, lighting, and a healthy diet. When these living conditions prevail, the dragons will rarely ever get sick.

Feel-Good Climate

Bearded dragons are cold-blooded (poikilothermic) animals. They are unable to adjust their body temperatures independently, which then correspond largely to the ambient temperature surrounding the animals (i.e., in the terrarium).

Warmth means life During low ambient temperatures, the body functions of bearded dragons are substantially reduced; however, with sufficient warmth, their metabolism works at full speed. Only then can the animals react quickly enough to hunt successfully and ensure that their digestive systems function. The immune system of bearded dragons is also temperature dependent. Bearded dragons that

are forced to live for an extended period in a cool terrarium do not have adequate (immune) defenses, and soon start to lose body condition and get sick. Preferred temperature range: 82 to 91°F (28 to 33°C).

Better dry Bearded dragons come from a rather dry environment with a narrow bacterial flora. An elevated humidity is harmful to their health, since pathogens flourish in such an environment. Optimum humidity: 40% during the day, 50 to 60% at night.

Fresh air Good ventilation is very important in a terrarium. Under humid conditions, the dragon's growth becomes stunted.

Healthy sleep The winter dormancy period (see page 52) is essential. It fortifies the body system, extends the longevity, and triggers the reproductive mood of the animals.

UV Lighting Makes Fit

More light As typical desert and steppe inhabitants, bearded dragons only feel well in brightly illuminated terrariums. In addition, hunting success is very much dependent upon ambient brightness.

UV for fitness Bearded dragons can perceive UV light. UV radiation in a terrarium promotes the well-being, and vitamin D3 synthesis is only possible under exposure to UV-B-light.

Sunbathing During the summer months, you should offer your bearded dragon regular outdoor exposure to sunbathing if possible. An artificial UV source is absolutely needed otherwise.

Many bearded dragons enjoy an extensive bath. The water level must not be too high.

Preventing Diseases

› Provide a balanced diet. A diverse offering of plant foods and live animals prevents malnutrition.
› Avoid stress. The size of the terrarium must fit the number and sizes of animals kept and should contain a large number of suitable hiding places. All occupants should be of about the same size.
› Pay attention to hygiene. Replace drinking water daily, and disinfect the drinking bowl every 4 weeks.

Remove fecal matter immediately; the bottom substrate should be completely replaced once or twice a year. Each terrarium should have its own feeding forceps and feces removal scoop.
› Precautions. Check fecal material for parasite infestation before the onset of winter dormancy. Locate a veterinarian with reptile experience BEFORE you actually purchase bearded dragons.

1 DRINKING HABITS Although bearded dragons come from arid regions, they must have constant access to fresh and clean water. They like to drink copious volumes. Not all specimens will learn to take water from a drink container. Many lick water droplets that have previously been sprayed throughout the terrarium. Sometimes dragons also take water given by hand. The water bowl is often also used for bathing.

2 MAINTAINING A SLIM FIGURE If fed in excess, bearded dragons have a tendency to gain weight rapidly. With two fasting days per week and a lot of vegetarian food (ratio of plant and animal food approximately 1 : 1) the dragons remain slender and healthy. A variable diet is the basis of balanced nutrition.

3 INDIVIDUAL FEEDING Animals at the bottom of the hierarchy often miss out on food. In that case, they should be fed individually by hand using forceps. This method is also advantageous when feeding cockroaches, so that the insects are not running around uncontrolled in the terrarium. Do not let the dragons bite the forceps, because that could damage their teeth.

When Bearded Dragons Get Sick

The most common causes for illnesses among bearded dragons are vitamin and mineral deficiencies, stress, and inadequate care and maintenance conditions.

Bone Diseases

Metabolism-related diseases of the bony skeleton are caused by an insufficient supply of vitamin D3 and an unfavorable calcium-phosphorus ratio. The calcium component must be higher than that of phosphorus (2 : 1 or 3 : 1), as found in the diet of wild dragons but not in a terrarium, where commercially acquired food animals contain more phosphorus than calcium. Growing dragons can come down with a rickets-like disease that affects the entire bony skeleton, especially the vertebral column, jaw, and tail. In part, bones are significantly deformed, which leads to severe impairment of mobility, and is irreparable.

Preventative measures Metabolic-related bone diseases can be prevented with a quality vitamin-

mineral powder (e.g., Korvimin ZVTReptil or similar product, upon veterinary advice), a variable diet, and daily use of a UVA/UVB light source. A veterinarian must treat animals that are already sick.

Molting Problems

Molting difficulties can occur as a result of an undersupply of vitamins, general weakness (following an illness), or having been kept too cold or too dry. The animals will molt only partially or not at all. Under the old skin, inflammations can occur, or the skin will simply dry up, shrink, and then severely constrict toes or the tip of the tail so that these atrophy. A stay of several hours in a very wet terrarium will soak the old skin so that it can then be peeled off with a pair of forceps. However, you must never use force!

Preventative measures Temperature, humidity, and diet must be adapted to their needs.

Egg Binding

Egg binding occurs when a gravid female cannot deposit her eggs. The trigger mechanism for this condition can be nonavailability of a suitable place for depositing the eggs, stress arising from interaction with other bearded dragons in the same terrarium, lack of calcium, or some weakness-induced disease.

At the very least, a veterinarian needs to be consulted when the egg-laying due date has been substantially exceeded, or when the female is becoming

This *P. vitticeps* is not fit due to poor care. It has become stuck in its old skin.

Frequent Diseases and Injuries

NAME	DESCRIPTION AND THERAPY	NAME	DESCRIPTION AND THERAPY
FRACTURES	Due to injuries and bites. Should be treated by a veterinarian. Fractures in reptiles heal fairly quickly.	GOUT	Insufficient moisture uptake. Urine salt deposits in joints and kidneys. Prevention: encourage maximum drinking.
BITES	Disinfect wounds, accommodation on clean substrate in quarantine tank. Consult veterinarian if wounds are infected.	ULCERATED STOMATITIS	Bacterial infection following injury in the jaw region, inflammation, and swelling, followed by development of tumor. Bony tissue is being destroyed. Timely diagnosis is vital, therapy by veterinarian. Prevention: strengthening of immune defenses by species-correct care and proper diet.
BURNS	From heat lamp or heater. Shield the heat source. Treat small burns with appropriate ointment, larger ones should be attended to by veterinarian.		
FATTY LIVER	Excessive, one-sided nutrition (e.g., insects only). Prevention: a balanced diet and two fasting days per week for adult specimens.	SKIN FUNGI	When kept too moist, encrustations develop especially on feet and legs. Diagnoses by veterinarian; treatment with antibiotics. Prevention: optimize holding facility, administer vitamin A.
BONE DISEASES	Vitamin D3 deficiency and incorrect calcium-phosphorus supply leads to a rickets-like disease in young specimens, and in adults to osteomalacia. Prevention: vitamin-mineral preparation supplement, balanced diet, UV lighting.	ENDO-PARASITES	These are, among others, worms and unicellular organisms. Symptoms: loss of condition, bloodied and slimy feces, apathy, pale coloration. Contagious with quick progression toward ultimate death. Diagnosis by veterinarian based on blood smears or fecal sample. Repeated treatment and disinfection of terrarium required. Some parasites can be transmitted to humans.
MOLTING PROBLEMS	Animals are kept too dry or too cold, in poor general condition or vitamin deficiency. Prevention: improve climate in terrarium, feed balanced diet.		
ECTO-PARASITES	Attack of skin by mites and ticks around eyes, ears, and arm and leg pits and in the cloacal region. Parasites can be seen with the naked eye. Removal with forceps or insecticides recommended by veterinarian; disinfect entire terrarium.	PNEUMONIA	When dragons are kept too cold and too damp. Foaming at the mouth, discharge from mouth and nostrils. Therapy by a veterinarian. Prevention: improve holding conditions.

increasingly unsettled and starts digging at many different sites in the terrarium. The veterinarian will be
trying to induce egg laying by administering calcium
and a uterotonic agent. If that does not work, the
eggs will be removed by means of a cesarean section.
It is not uncommon for egg binding to become fatal,
unless treated promptly. Even if the female does not
survive, it is often possible to save the eggs.

Bite Injuries

Bite injuries occur principally among young bearded
dragons that are being raised within a group. Most
commonly involved are the legs and particularly the
tip of the tail. Responsible for these injuries is the
innate hunting instinct of these inexperienced animals, which—at that stage of their lives—will bite at
anything that moves, whereby wiggling tips of tails
represent particularly potent stimuli. Juveniles with
permanently damaged tails are no rarity. This condition hardly interferes with the animals, but it does not
look particularly attractive. If the tail section has been
bitten clear through, the wounds will heal quickly.
As a precautionary measure, it should be treated with
a wound disinfectant, and the animal placed into a
quarantine tank for a few days, where newspaper is
used instead of regular substrate. During subsequent
molting, it is important to check whether there are
any skin remnants left behind on the body of the
dragon. Veterinary attention is required in the event
that the tail is only partially bitten through, or has
been crushed or when possibly decay has set in.
Preventative measures Bite injuries can be
largely prevented when young bearded dragons are
kept in small groups only and are given an abun-
dant amount of food. There should always be a few
food animals remaining in the terrarium.

A wild common bearded dragon in its native
Australian environment is sunbathing, while over-
looking its territory from an elevated vantage point.

A Matter for the **Veterinarian**

SURGICAL OPERATION Operations and similar
surgical procedures on bearded dragons must only
be made by a veterinarian. He or she establishes
the diagnosis and proceeds with a treatment that
is as painless as possible.

EUTHANASIA Relevant animal welfare laws pro-
hibit the use of euthanasia of terminally ill reptiles
in a freezer compartment, a method that is very
painful to the animals. Only a veterinarian is allo-
wed to put a reptile to sleep.

EXPERIENCE Before you purchase your bearded
dragon, you should make inquiries to find a veterinarian that has experience in the treatment of reptiles. Suitable veterinarians in your vicinity can be
found on the Internet (see Resources, page 62).

Checking for Parasites

A fecal sample can provide information whether a dragon has internal parasites. Such a check is particularly important prior to the winter dormancy phase.

Taking a Sample

Even bearded dragons are not immune against endoparasites. Some endoparasites can cause many problems, but others may not be harmful or may aid in the digestive process. There are those, however, that can be serious and even fatal. The digestive tract is the most commonly affected organ.

› Many parasites or their eggs are excreted via feces and can be readily detected.

› If you collect feces, this should be as fresh as possible and preferably from a clean substrate, such as paper.

› Urine containers (available from drugstores, etc.) are very suitable for carrying or mailing feces samples. During periods of hot weather, a few drops of water will prevent the sample from drying up. Use a separate container for each fecal sample. The container should be properly labeled, and an accompanying written description provides information about animal species and disease symptoms.

Findings

Fecal samples are generally analyzed by various facilities. Normally, a veterinarian will make all necessary arrangements, and in many instances, he/she will do the examination in-house. Alternately, the veterinarian may be able to advise you of other laboratory facilities that can examine fecal samples from reptiles. Once results have been obtained, the veterinarian will provide you with appropriate treatment recommendations. A single sample without specific findings does not provide total assurance that parasites are not being continuously excreted. Even dead bearded dragons should be examined in the interest of the health of the other terrarium inhabitants. Apart from the cause of death, the examination results generally also provide information about husbandry mistakes, such as overfeeding the animals or keeping them too dry. The body of a dead animal must be submitted for autopsy/examination within 24 hours in refrigerated (not frozen) condition to your veterinarian or to some other investigating facility (veterinary laboratory, etc.).

Even for a heat-resistant bearded dragon, it can get too hot in an outdoor enclosure. Therefore, a shaded area is necessary and always very welcome.

INDEX

Herpetological Societies

› Herpetologist's League
c/o Texas National Heritage Program
Texas Parks and Wildlife Department
4200 Smith School Road
Austin, TX 78744

› Society for the Study of Amphibians and Reptiles (SAR)
Department of Zoology
Miami University
Oxford, OH 45056

Bearded Dragons on the Internet

› www.bearded-dragons.com/
› www.beardeddragonguide.com/
› www.caresheet.com/bearded_dragon.html
› www.hotfrog.com/Products/Bearded-Dragons
› www.mypets.net.au/flex/articles/197/bearded-dragons-.cfm
› www.terrariums.com/terrariums/terrariumfaqsarticle.cfm

Books

› Bartlett, Richard D. and Patricia P. *Reptile and Ampibian Keeper's Guide: Bearded Dragons.* Barron's Educational Series, Inc., 2009.
› Mader, Douglas R. *Reptile Medicine and Surgery*, 2nd Ed. Saunders Elsevier, 2006.

Periodicals

› *Herpetological Review* and *Journal of Herpetology*
Society for the Study of Amphibians and Reptiles
P.O. Box 58517
Salt Lake City, UT 84158

› *Reptiles*
P.O. Box 6050
Mission Viejo, CA 92690

Acknowledgment

The publishers, author, and photographer would like to express their gratitude to **Michaela** and **Friedhelm Steffen**, Fressnapf Warburg, **Frank Hose**, Zoohaus-Süd, Kassel, **Das Chamäleonhaus**, Mühlheim am Main, and to **Richard Thornton**, Paderborn.

Important Notes

› Diseases Some reptile diseases can be transmitted to humans. Wash your hands thoroughly after handling the animals and servicing the terrarium.

› Health Check Have your animals checked regularly, preferably just before their winter dormancy.

› Electrical Equipment Working with electrical equipment and cables always presents a potential risk. All equipment items must carry an official safety inspection label. Defective equipment must be replaced immediately.

The title of the German book is *Bartagamen*

English translation by U. Erich Friese

All inquiries should be addressed to:
Barron's Educational Series, Inc.
250 Wireless Boulevard
Hauppauge, NY 11788
www.barronseduc.com

ISBN-13: 978-0-7641-4286-4
ISBN-10: 0-7641-4286-0

Library of Congress Control No.: 2009010417

Library of Congress Cataloging-in-Publication Data
Au, Manfred.
    [Bartagamen. English]
    Bearded dragons / author, Manfred Au; photographer,
Christine Steimer.
        p. cm.
    Includes bibliographical references and index.
    ISBN-13: 978-0-7641-4286-4
    ISBN 10. 0 7641 4286 0
1. Bearded dragons (Reptiles) as pets. I. Title.

    SF459.L5A9613 2009
    639.3'955—dc22   2009010417

PRINTED IN CHINA
9 8 7 6 5 4 3 2 1

The Author

Manfred Au has been keeping terrariums
for 30 years. In 1983 he was one of the
first in Germany to breed the Common
Bearded Dragon, *Pogona vitticeps*, regularly.
During the following years he also bred
P. henrylawsoni, *P. barbata*, and *P. mitchelli*.
Today, he is principally interested in geckos
and chameleons.

The Photographers

Christine Steimer works as a freelance
photographer and is specializing in pet
photography. She works for international
publishing houses, specialist journals, and
advertising agencies.

David Fischer lives in New South Wales,
Australia. He has been involved with field
herpetology for many years, and he is
known for his impressive animal and
nature photographs.

Photo References

All photographs by Christine Steimer,
except for: David Fischer: p. 6, 8, 9, 16
top, 17 top, 58; Fotoagentur Auscape:
p. 16 center.

SOS – What to do?

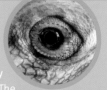

Leg Fracture

PROBLEM: The dragon has a broken leg. **THIS COULD HELP:** The fracture has to be set and placed in a cast by a veterinarian. Immobilization does not pose a problem during walking. Healing in bearded dragons is—as in all reptiles—fairly rapid.

Flaking Skin

PROBLEM: Loose pieces of skin. **THIS COULD HELP:** The outer layer of skin in reptiles is dead and cannot grow. It is continuously replaced by a new, larger one. Normally bearded dragons do not require any help. If the old skin does not flake off, it must be soaked and carefully removed with forceps.

Loss of Appetite

PROBLEM: Although they are given their favorite food, the dragons will not eat. **THIS COULD HELP:** At the onset of winter, this behavior is quite normal. The lizards prepare themselves for the winter dormancy period. They start to withdraw and will no longer feed.

Claws Too Long

PROBLEM: The bearded dragon has problems running, because the claws on its legs have become too long, causing mobility problems. **THIS COULD HELP:** The claws will have to be trimmed back. Caution: The tiny blood vessels in each claw must not be damaged. Your veterinarian will show you the correct cutting procedure.

Weight Gain

PROBLEM: The female eats more than normal and is getting "fatter." **THIS COULD HELP:** The dragon is gravid and now requires a lot of quality food for proper egg development.

Alarm Signal

PROBLEM: The eyes of the bearded lizards have sunken in deeply and are mostly closed. The lizard acts lethargic. **THIS COULD HELP:** The eyes of healthy animals are clear and protrude slightly from the eye socket. Inactive behavior is always an alarm signal. A lizard as the one described above should be taken to a veterinarian immediately.